45 Hungarian Recipes for Home

By: Kelly Johnson

Table of Contents

Soups:

- Goulash Soup
- Jókai Bean Soup
- Fisherman's Soup (Halászlé)
- Chicken Paprikash Soup
- Lebbencs Soup (Hungarian Lentil Soup)

Main Dishes:

- Chicken Paprikash
- Hungarian Beef Goulash
- Lecsó (Pepper and Tomato Stew)
- Hortobágyi Palacsinta (Savory Pancakes with Meat)
- Stuffed Peppers (Töltött Paprika)
- Pörkölt (Meat Stew)
- Rakott Krumpli (Layered Potatoes)
- Tojásos Nokedli (Noodles with Eggs)
- Túrós Csusza (Noodles with Curd)

Side Dishes:

- Hungarian Cucumber Salad (Uborkasaláta)
- Káposztasaláta (Cabbage Salad)
- Hungarian Red Cabbage
- Paprika Potatoes
- Lángos (Fried Bread)
- Krumpli Saláta (Potato Salad)

Desserts:

- Dobos Torte
- Hungarian Nut Roll (Diós Beigli)
- Kürtőskalács (Chimney Cake)
- Rákóczi Túrós (Cottage Cheese Cake)
- Rétes (Strudel) - Apple or Cherry
- Somlói Galuska (Chocolate Sponge Cake)

- Gesztenyepüré (Chestnut Puree)

Pastries and Breads:

- Pogácsa (Cheese Biscuits)
- Kifli (Nut or Poppy Seed Crescent Rolls)
- Zsemle (Soft White Rolls)
- Lángos (Deep-Fried Flatbread)
- Diós Kalács (Walnut Bread)

Drinks:

- Pálinka (Fruit Brandy)
- Unicum (Herbal Liqueur)
- Fröccs (Wine Spritzer)
- Palinka Sour

Snacks:

- Tökmag (Roasted Pumpkin Seeds)
- Túrós Rudi (Chocolate-Covered Cottage Cheese Bars)
- Pogácsa (Savory Scones)
- Túró Rudi Mousse

Breakfast:

- Rakott Krumpli (Layered Potatoes with Eggs)
- Hungarian Omelette
- Túróscsusza (Noodles with Curd)

Holiday Specialties:

- Beigli (Christmas Poppy Seed and Walnut Roll)
- Szaloncukor (Christmas Candy)

Soups:

Goulash Soup

Ingredients:

- 2 lbs (900g) beef stew meat, cut into bite-sized cubes
- 2 large onions, finely chopped
- 2 cloves garlic, minced
- 2 tbsp vegetable oil
- 2 tbsp sweet Hungarian paprika
- 1 tsp caraway seeds
- 1 tsp dried marjoram
- 1 bay leaf
- 2 large potatoes, peeled and diced
- 2 carrots, peeled and sliced
- 1 bell pepper, diced
- 1 can (14 oz/400g) diced tomatoes
- 4 cups beef broth
- Salt and pepper to taste
- Fresh parsley, chopped, for garnish
- Sour cream, for serving

Instructions:

In a large pot, heat the vegetable oil over medium heat. Add the chopped onions and sauté until translucent.
Add the minced garlic and continue to sauté for another minute until fragrant.
Add the beef cubes to the pot and brown them on all sides. Season with salt and pepper.
Stir in the sweet Hungarian paprika, caraway seeds, and dried marjoram. Cook for an additional 2-3 minutes to allow the flavors to meld.
Pour in the diced tomatoes, beef broth, and add the bay leaf. Bring the mixture to a boil, then reduce the heat to low and let it simmer for 1-2 hours or until the beef is tender.
Add the diced potatoes, sliced carrots, and diced bell pepper to the pot. Continue simmering until the vegetables are cooked through.
Adjust the seasoning with salt and pepper according to taste.

Remove the bay leaf from the soup.
Serve the Goulash Soup hot, garnished with chopped fresh parsley, and with a dollop of sour cream on top.

Enjoy this hearty and flavorful Hungarian Goulash Soup!

Jókai Bean Soup

Ingredients:

- 1 cup dried pinto beans, soaked overnight
- 1 onion, finely chopped
- 2 cloves garlic, minced
- 2 tbsp vegetable oil
- 1 Hungarian wax pepper or mild chili pepper, diced
- 1/2 lb (225g) smoked sausage, sliced
- 1/2 lb (225g) smoked ham, diced
- 1 tomato, diced
- 1 tbsp sweet Hungarian paprika
- 1 tsp ground cumin
- 1 bay leaf
- 6 cups chicken or vegetable broth
- Salt and pepper to taste
- Fresh parsley, chopped, for garnish
- Sour cream, for serving

Instructions:

Rinse the soaked beans and set them aside.
In a large pot, heat the vegetable oil over medium heat. Add the chopped onions and sauté until translucent.
Add the minced garlic and diced pepper to the pot, continuing to sauté for another minute.
Stir in the smoked sausage and ham, cooking until they begin to brown.
Add the diced tomato, sweet Hungarian paprika, and ground cumin to the pot. Cook for an additional 2-3 minutes.
Pour in the soaked beans and chicken or vegetable broth. Add the bay leaf. Bring the mixture to a boil, then reduce the heat to low and let it simmer for 1.5 to 2 hours or until the beans are tender.
Season the soup with salt and pepper according to taste.
Once the beans are fully cooked, remove the bay leaf from the soup.
Serve the Jókai Bean Soup hot, garnished with chopped fresh parsley, and with a dollop of sour cream on top.

Enjoy the rich flavors of Jókai Bean Soup, a classic Hungarian dish!

Fisherman's Soup (Halászlé)

Ingredients:

- 2 lbs (900g) mixed freshwater fish (carp, catfish, perch), cleaned and cut into chunks
- 1 large onion, finely chopped
- 2 cloves garlic, minced
- 2 tbsp vegetable oil
- 2 Hungarian wax peppers or mild chili peppers, finely chopped
- 2 tomatoes, diced
- 1 tbsp sweet Hungarian paprika
- 1 tsp hot Hungarian paprika (adjust to taste)
- 1 bay leaf
- Salt and pepper to taste
- 1/2 cup dry white wine
- 6 cups fish or vegetable broth
- Fresh parsley, chopped, for garnish
- Lemon wedges, for serving

Instructions:

In a large pot, heat the vegetable oil over medium heat. Add the chopped onions and sauté until translucent.
Add the minced garlic and diced peppers to the pot, continuing to sauté for another minute.
Stir in the diced tomatoes, sweet Hungarian paprika, and hot Hungarian paprika. Cook for an additional 2-3 minutes.
Add the chunks of fish to the pot and gently mix to coat them with the spices.
Pour in the white wine and let it simmer for a few minutes to reduce and burn off the alcohol.
Add the fish or vegetable broth to the pot. Place the bay leaf into the mixture.
Bring the soup to a boil, then reduce the heat to low and let it simmer for about 20-30 minutes until the fish is cooked through.
Season the soup with salt and pepper according to taste.
Remove the bay leaf from the soup.
Serve the Fisherman's Soup hot, garnished with chopped fresh parsley, and with lemon wedges on the side.

Enjoy the delicious flavors of Hungarian Fisherman's Soup!

Chicken Paprikash Soup

Ingredients:

- 2 lbs (900g) chicken thighs, bone-in, skin-on
- Salt and pepper to taste
- 2 tbsp vegetable oil
- 1 large onion, finely chopped
- 2 cloves garlic, minced
- 2 tbsp sweet Hungarian paprika
- 1 tsp hot Hungarian paprika (adjust to taste)
- 1 bell pepper, diced
- 1 tomato, diced
- 6 cups chicken broth
- 1 bay leaf
- 1 cup egg noodles or dumplings
- 1 cup sour cream
- Fresh parsley, chopped, for garnish

Instructions:

Season the chicken thighs with salt and pepper.
In a large pot, heat the vegetable oil over medium heat. Add the chicken thighs, and brown them on all sides. Remove chicken from the pot and set aside.
In the same pot, add chopped onions and sauté until translucent. Add minced garlic and sauté for an additional minute.
Stir in the sweet Hungarian paprika and hot Hungarian paprika. Cook for 2-3 minutes to release the flavors.
Add diced bell pepper and tomato to the pot. Cook for another 3-5 minutes until the vegetables soften.
Return the browned chicken thighs to the pot. Pour in the chicken broth and add the bay leaf. Bring the mixture to a boil, then reduce the heat to low and let it simmer for 30-40 minutes until the chicken is cooked through.
Meanwhile, prepare the egg noodles or dumplings according to the package instructions. Add them to the soup during the last 10 minutes of cooking.
Once the chicken is cooked, remove it from the pot, shred the meat, and return it to the soup.
Stir in sour cream, and let the soup simmer for an additional 5-10 minutes.

Adjust the seasoning with salt and pepper according to taste.
Serve the Chicken Paprikash Soup hot, garnished with chopped fresh parsley.

Enjoy this comforting and flavorful Hungarian soup!

Lebbencs Soup (Hungarian Lentil Soup)

Ingredients:

- 1 cup green or brown lentils, rinsed and drained
- 2 tbsp vegetable oil
- 1 onion, finely chopped
- 2 carrots, diced
- 2 celery stalks, diced
- 2 cloves garlic, minced
- 2 potatoes, peeled and diced
- 1 bay leaf
- 1 tsp sweet Hungarian paprika
- 1/2 tsp caraway seeds
- 6 cups vegetable or chicken broth
- Salt and pepper to taste
- Fresh parsley, chopped, for garnish
- Sour cream, for serving

Instructions:

In a large pot, heat the vegetable oil over medium heat. Add the chopped onion, carrots, and celery. Sauté until the vegetables are softened.
Add minced garlic to the pot and sauté for an additional minute.
Stir in sweet Hungarian paprika and caraway seeds, allowing the spices to release their flavors.
Add lentils, diced potatoes, and bay leaf to the pot. Pour in the vegetable or chicken broth.
Bring the mixture to a boil, then reduce the heat to low. Cover and simmer for about 30-40 minutes, or until the lentils and vegetables are tender.
Season the soup with salt and pepper according to taste.
Remove the bay leaf from the soup.
Serve the Hungarian Lentil Soup hot, garnished with chopped fresh parsley, and with a dollop of sour cream on top.

Enjoy this hearty and nutritious Lentil Soup inspired by Hungarian flavors!

Main Dishes:

Chicken Paprikash

Ingredients:

- 4 chicken thighs, bone-in, skin-on
- Salt and pepper to taste
- 2 tbsp vegetable oil
- 1 large onion, finely chopped
- 2 cloves garlic, minced
- 2 tbsp sweet Hungarian paprika
- 1 tsp hot Hungarian paprika (adjust to taste)
- 1 cup chicken broth
- 1 cup diced tomatoes (fresh or canned)
- 1 bell pepper, sliced
- 1 cup sour cream
- 2 tbsp all-purpose flour (for thickening)
- 1 tsp caraway seeds (optional)
- Fresh parsley, chopped, for garnish
- Egg noodles or rice, for serving

Instructions:

Season the chicken thighs with salt and pepper.
In a large, deep skillet or Dutch oven, heat the vegetable oil over medium-high heat. Add the chicken thighs and brown them on all sides. Remove chicken from the pot and set aside.
In the same pot, add chopped onions and sauté until translucent. Add minced garlic and sauté for an additional minute.
Stir in the sweet Hungarian paprika and hot Hungarian paprika. Cook for 2-3 minutes to release the flavors.
Return the browned chicken thighs to the pot. Add chicken broth, diced tomatoes, and bell pepper. If using, sprinkle caraway seeds over the top. Bring the mixture to a boil, then reduce the heat to low, cover, and simmer for about 30-40 minutes or until the chicken is cooked through.
In a small bowl, mix sour cream and flour to create a smooth paste. Stir this mixture into the pot, ensuring it is well incorporated.

Simmer for an additional 10-15 minutes, stirring occasionally, until the sauce thickens.
Adjust the seasoning with salt and pepper according to taste.
Serve the Chicken Paprikash over egg noodles or rice, garnished with chopped fresh parsley.

Enjoy this delicious and comforting Hungarian Chicken Paprikash!

Hungarian Beef Goulash

Ingredients:

- 2 lbs (900g) beef stew meat, cut into bite-sized cubes
- Salt and pepper to taste
- 3 tbsp vegetable oil
- 2 large onions, finely chopped
- 2 cloves garlic, minced
- 3 tbsp sweet Hungarian paprika
- 1 tsp hot Hungarian paprika (adjust to taste)
- 1 tbsp tomato paste
- 2 bell peppers, diced
- 2 tomatoes, diced
- 2 bay leaves
- 2 tsp caraway seeds
- 4 cups beef broth
- 3 large potatoes, peeled and diced
- Chopped fresh parsley, for garnish

Instructions:

Season the beef cubes with salt and pepper.
In a large pot or Dutch oven, heat the vegetable oil over medium-high heat. Add the beef cubes and brown them on all sides. Work in batches if needed, to avoid overcrowding the pot.
Remove the browned beef from the pot and set it aside.
In the same pot, add chopped onions and sauté until translucent. Add minced garlic and sauté for an additional minute.
Stir in sweet Hungarian paprika, hot Hungarian paprika, and tomato paste. Cook for 2-3 minutes to release the flavors.
Add diced bell peppers, tomatoes, bay leaves, and caraway seeds to the pot. Cook for another 5 minutes.
Return the browned beef to the pot and pour in the beef broth. Bring the mixture to a boil, then reduce the heat to low, cover, and let it simmer for about 1.5 to 2 hours or until the beef is tender.
Add the diced potatoes to the pot and continue simmering until the potatoes are cooked through.

Adjust the seasoning with salt and pepper according to taste.
Serve the Hungarian Beef Goulash hot, garnished with chopped fresh parsley.

Enjoy this classic and comforting Hungarian dish! Serve it with crusty bread or over egg noodles.

Lecsó (Pepper and Tomato Stew)

Ingredients:

- 2 tablespoons vegetable oil
- 1 onion, finely chopped
- 2-3 cloves garlic, minced
- 4-5 Hungarian wax peppers or bell peppers, diced
- 4-5 ripe tomatoes, chopped (or 1 can of diced tomatoes)
- 1 teaspoon sweet paprika
- Salt and pepper to taste
- Optional: Hungarian hot paprika for extra heat
- 2-3 Hungarian sausage links or chorizo, sliced (optional)
- Fresh parsley or cilantro, chopped, for garnish

Instructions:

In a large skillet or pan, heat the vegetable oil over medium heat.
Add the finely chopped onion and minced garlic. Sauté until the onion becomes translucent.
Add the diced peppers to the skillet and continue to sauté for a few minutes until they start to soften.
Add the chopped tomatoes (or canned tomatoes) to the pan. Stir well.
Season the mixture with sweet paprika, salt, and pepper. If you like it spicy, you can also add Hungarian hot paprika for extra heat.
If using, add the sliced Hungarian sausage or chorizo to the pan and cook until browned.
Cover the skillet and let the ingredients simmer over low to medium heat for about 20-30 minutes, stirring occasionally.
Taste and adjust the seasoning if needed.
Once the peppers are tender and the flavors have melded, the Lecsó is ready.
Garnish with chopped fresh parsley or cilantro before serving.
Serve Lecsó hot, typically as a main course with bread, rice, or pasta.

Lecsó is a versatile dish, and variations exist across different regions and households.

Feel free to customize it according to your taste, and enjoy this comforting Hungarian pepper and tomato stew!

Hortobágyi Palacsinta (Savory Pancakes with Meat)

Ingredients:

For the Pancakes:

- 1 cup all-purpose flour
- 1 1/2 cups milk
- 2 eggs
- Pinch of salt
- Vegetable oil for frying

For the Meat Filling:

- 1 onion, finely chopped
- 1 tablespoon vegetable oil
- 1 pound ground meat (beef, pork, or a mixture)
- 1 teaspoon sweet paprika
- Salt and pepper to taste
- 2 tablespoons tomato paste
- 1 cup beef or vegetable broth
- 1 tablespoon all-purpose flour (for thickening)
- 1/2 cup sour cream

For Garnish:

- Chopped fresh parsley

Instructions:

In a mixing bowl, whisk together the flour, milk, eggs, and a pinch of salt to make the pancake batter. Let it rest for about 15 minutes.
In a non-stick skillet, heat a small amount of vegetable oil over medium heat. Pour a ladle of the pancake batter into the skillet, swirling it to spread evenly. Cook the pancake on both sides until golden brown. Repeat until all the batter is used.

In a separate pan, sauté the finely chopped onion in vegetable oil until translucent.
Add the ground meat to the onions and cook until browned.
Season the meat with sweet paprika, salt, and pepper.
Stir in the tomato paste and cook for a couple of minutes.
In a small bowl, mix the flour with a bit of water to create a slurry. Add it to the meat mixture.
Pour in the broth and simmer until the mixture thickens.
Remove the pan from heat, and stir in the sour cream. Adjust the seasoning if needed.
Place a generous spoonful of the meat filling onto each pancake, spreading it evenly. Roll the pancakes or fold them into squares.
Arrange the filled pancakes in a baking dish.
Optionally, you can bake the filled pancakes in the oven for a few minutes to heat through.
Garnish with chopped fresh parsley before serving.

Hortobágyi palacsinta is often served with a dollop of sour cream on top. Enjoy these savory Hungarian pancakes as a satisfying main dish!

Stuffed Peppers (Töltött Paprika)

Ingredients:

For the Stuffed Peppers:

- 6 large bell peppers (green, red, or yellow)
- 1 cup rice, cooked
- 1 pound ground meat (beef, pork, or a mixture)
- 1 onion, finely chopped
- 2 cloves garlic, minced
- 1 egg
- 1 tablespoon sweet paprika
- Salt and pepper to taste
- 1 cup tomato sauce or crushed tomatoes
- 1 cup beef or vegetable broth
- Fresh parsley, chopped, for garnish

For the Tomato Sauce:

- 2 cups tomato sauce or crushed tomatoes
- 1 tablespoon sweet paprika
- Salt and sugar to taste

Instructions:

Preheat the oven to 375°F (190°C).
Cut the tops off the bell peppers and remove the seeds and membranes.
In a large mixing bowl, combine the cooked rice, ground meat, chopped onion, minced garlic, egg, sweet paprika, salt, and pepper. Mix well until all ingredients are evenly combined.
Stuff each bell pepper with the meat and rice mixture, pressing it down gently.
In a separate bowl, mix together the ingredients for the tomato sauce – tomato sauce or crushed tomatoes, sweet paprika, salt, and a pinch of sugar to balance the acidity.
Place the stuffed peppers in a baking dish.
Pour the tomato sauce over the stuffed peppers.
Pour the beef or vegetable broth into the bottom of the baking dish.
Cover the baking dish with aluminum foil.

Bake in the preheated oven for about 60-75 minutes or until the peppers are tender.
Occasionally baste the peppers with the juices from the bottom of the baking dish to keep them moist.
Remove from the oven and let them rest for a few minutes.
Garnish with chopped fresh parsley before serving.

Serve the Stuffed Peppers hot, drizzled with the tomato sauce from the baking dish. This dish is often enjoyed with a side of crusty bread or a dollop of sour cream.

Pörkölt (Meat Stew)

Ingredients:

- 2 tablespoons lard or vegetable oil
- 2 onions, finely chopped
- 2 cloves garlic, minced
- 2 pounds (about 1 kg) beef stew meat, cut into bite-sized pieces
- 2 tablespoons sweet paprika
- 1 teaspoon caraway seeds
- Salt and black pepper to taste
- 2 tomatoes, chopped (or 1 cup crushed tomatoes)
- 1 red bell pepper, diced
- 1 green bell pepper, diced
- 2 tablespoons tomato paste
- 2 cups beef broth
- 1 bay leaf
- 1 teaspoon dried marjoram
- 1 teaspoon thyme (optional)
- 1 tablespoon flour (optional, for thickening)
- Chopped fresh parsley, for garnish
- Sour cream, for serving (optional)

Instructions:

In a large pot or Dutch oven, heat the lard or vegetable oil over medium heat.
Add the finely chopped onions and sauté until translucent.
Stir in the minced garlic and cook for an additional minute until fragrant.
Add the beef stew meat to the pot, and brown the meat on all sides.
Sprinkle sweet paprika, caraway seeds, salt, and black pepper over the meat. Mix well to coat the meat with the spices.
Add the chopped tomatoes, diced red and green bell peppers, and tomato paste. Stir to combine.
Pour in the beef broth and add the bay leaf, dried marjoram, and thyme (if using).
Bring the mixture to a simmer, then reduce the heat to low, cover the pot, and let it cook for about 1.5 to 2 hours or until the meat is tender.
If you prefer a thicker stew, you can make a roux by mixing 1 tablespoon of flour with a bit of water and stirring it into the pot. Cook for an additional 10-15 minutes.

Adjust the seasoning if needed.
Remove the bay leaf before serving.
Garnish with chopped fresh parsley.
Serve Pörkölt hot, traditionally with a side of egg noodles, rice, or potatoes.
Optionally, you can add a dollop of sour cream on top.

Enjoy this hearty and flavorful Hungarian Beef Pörkölt!

Rakott Krumpli (Layered Potatoes)

Ingredients:

- 2 pounds (about 1 kg) potatoes, peeled and sliced into 1/4-inch rounds
- 4 hard-boiled eggs, sliced
- 1/2 pound (about 225g) Hungarian sausage or smoked sausage, thinly sliced
- 1 large onion, finely chopped
- 2 tablespoons vegetable oil or lard
- 2 tablespoons sweet paprika
- Salt and black pepper to taste
- 2 cups sour cream
- 1 cup grated cheese (Emmental, Gouda, or any melting cheese)
- Fresh parsley, chopped, for garnish

Instructions:

Preheat the oven to 375°F (190°C).
In a large pot, boil the sliced potatoes until they are just tender. Drain and set aside.
In a skillet, heat the vegetable oil or lard over medium heat. Add the chopped onion and sauté until translucent.
Add the sliced sausage to the skillet and cook until lightly browned.
Stir in the sweet paprika, salt, and black pepper. Cook for an additional minute until the spices are fragrant.
In a separate bowl, mix the sour cream with a pinch of salt.
Grease a baking dish with butter or oil.
Begin assembling the layers in the baking dish: a layer of sliced potatoes, followed by a layer of hard-boiled eggs, a layer of sausage and onions, and a generous drizzle of sour cream.
Repeat the layers until all the ingredients are used, finishing with a layer of potatoes on top.
Sprinkle the grated cheese evenly over the top layer of potatoes.
Bake in the preheated oven for about 30-40 minutes or until the cheese is melted and bubbly, and the top is golden brown.
Remove from the oven and let it rest for a few minutes.
Garnish with chopped fresh parsley before serving.

Serve Rakott Krumpli hot, and enjoy the layers of flavors and textures in this comforting Hungarian dish. It's a great option for a hearty family meal.

Tojásos Nokedli (Noodles with Eggs)

Ingredients:

For the Nokedli (Dumplings):

- 2 cups all-purpose flour
- 3 large eggs
- 1/2 cup water
- 1/2 teaspoon salt

For the Scrambled Eggs:

- 4 large eggs
- Salt and black pepper to taste
- 2 tablespoons butter or vegetable oil

Instructions:

In a large mixing bowl, combine the flour, eggs, water, and salt. Mix well until you have a smooth, thick batter. The consistency should be thicker than pancake batter.
Bring a large pot of salted water to boil.
Using a spaetzle maker, colander, or the back of a spoon, drop small portions of the batter into the boiling water. The dumplings will cook quickly and rise to the surface. Once they do, let them cook for an additional 1-2 minutes, then remove them with a slotted spoon and place them in a colander to drain.
In a large skillet, heat the butter or vegetable oil over medium heat.
Crack the eggs into a bowl, season with salt and black pepper, and whisk them together.
Pour the beaten eggs into the skillet with the melted butter or oil.
Stir the eggs gently as they cook, forming soft, scrambled curds.
Once the eggs are cooked to your liking, add the drained nokedli to the skillet.
Toss the nokedli with the scrambled eggs, ensuring they are well combined and heated through.
Adjust the seasoning if needed.
Serve Tojásos Nokedli hot, garnished with fresh herbs or green onions if desired.

Tojásos Nokedli is a simple and comforting dish, perfect for a quick meal. Enjoy the fluffy dumplings combined with the richness of scrambled eggs!

Túrós Csusza (Noodles with Curd)

Ingredients:

For the Egg Noodles:

- 2 cups all-purpose flour
- 2 large eggs
- 1/2 cup water
- 1/2 teaspoon salt

For the Curd Filling:

- 2 cups túró (Hungarian curd or farmer's cheese)
- 2 tablespoons butter
- 1/4 cup sour cream
- Salt to taste

For Garnish:

- Crispy bacon bits (optional)
- Chopped fresh parsley

Instructions:

In a large mixing bowl, combine the flour, eggs, water, and salt. Mix well until you have a smooth, thick batter. The consistency should be thicker than pancake batter.
Bring a large pot of salted water to boil.
Using a spaetzle maker, colander, or the back of a spoon, drop small portions of the batter into the boiling water. The noodles will cook quickly and rise to the surface. Once they do, let them cook for an additional 1-2 minutes, then remove them with a slotted spoon and place them in a colander to drain.
In a skillet, melt the butter over medium heat.
Add the túró (Hungarian curd or farmer's cheese) to the skillet. Stir gently until it starts to soften.

Mix in the sour cream and continue stirring until the curd is creamy and well combined with the sour cream.

Season the curd filling with salt to taste.

Add the cooked egg noodles to the skillet and toss them with the curd filling until well coated.

Optionally, garnish with crispy bacon bits and chopped fresh parsley for added flavor.

Serve Túrós Csusza hot, and enjoy the comforting combination of egg noodles and creamy curd!

Túrós Csusza is a classic Hungarian dish that showcases the simplicity and deliciousness of traditional ingredients.

Side Dishes:

Hungarian Cucumber Salad (Uborkasaláta)

Ingredients:

- 3 medium cucumbers, thinly sliced
- 1 small red onion, thinly sliced
- 1 cup sour cream
- 2 tablespoons white vinegar
- 1 tablespoon sugar
- 1 teaspoon salt
- Freshly ground black pepper, to taste
- Chopped fresh dill, for garnish

Instructions:

In a large bowl, combine the thinly sliced cucumbers and red onion.
In a separate bowl, whisk together the sour cream, white vinegar, sugar, salt, and black pepper until well combined.
Pour the sour cream mixture over the cucumbers and onions. Toss gently to coat the vegetables evenly.
Refrigerate the salad for at least 30 minutes to allow the flavors to meld and the salad to chill.
Before serving, garnish the Hungarian Cucumber Salad with chopped fresh dill for added freshness and flavor.
Serve chilled as a side dish with your favorite Hungarian meals.

Hungarian Cucumber Salad is a delightful side dish that complements the richness of many Hungarian dishes. Enjoy its crisp and tangy goodness!

Káposztasaláta (Cabbage Salad)

Ingredients:

- 1 small head of green cabbage, finely shredded
- 1 medium carrot, grated
- 1 small red onion, thinly sliced
- 1/4 cup white wine vinegar
- 1/4 cup vegetable oil
- 1 tablespoon sugar
- 1 teaspoon salt
- 1/2 teaspoon caraway seeds (optional)
- Freshly ground black pepper, to taste
- Chopped fresh parsley, for garnish

Instructions:

In a large mixing bowl, combine the finely shredded cabbage, grated carrot, and thinly sliced red onion.

In a small bowl, whisk together the white wine vinegar, vegetable oil, sugar, salt, and caraway seeds (if using).

Pour the dressing over the cabbage mixture and toss until the vegetables are evenly coated.

Season the salad with freshly ground black pepper to taste.

Allow the Káposztasaláta to marinate in the refrigerator for at least 30 minutes before serving to enhance the flavors.

Garnish with chopped fresh parsley before serving.

Serve chilled as a refreshing side dish with traditional Hungarian meals.

Hungarian Cabbage Salad adds a crisp and tangy element to the dining experience, making it a versatile and popular side dish. Enjoy its vibrant flavors!

Hungarian Red Cabbage

Ingredients:

- 1 medium-sized red cabbage, thinly sliced
- 1 large apple, peeled, cored, and grated
- 1 large onion, finely chopped
- 2 tablespoons vegetable oil or lard
- 2 tablespoons red wine vinegar
- 2 tablespoons sugar
- 1 teaspoon salt
- 1/2 teaspoon caraway seeds (optional)
- 1 cup water or vegetable broth

Instructions:

In a large pot or Dutch oven, heat the vegetable oil or lard over medium heat.
Add the finely chopped onion and sauté until translucent.
Add the thinly sliced red cabbage to the pot and continue to sauté for about 5-7 minutes until the cabbage begins to wilt.
Stir in the grated apple, red wine vinegar, sugar, salt, and caraway seeds (if using).
Pour in the water or vegetable broth to the pot, ensuring that the liquid covers the cabbage.
Bring the mixture to a simmer, then reduce the heat to low, cover the pot, and let it cook for approximately 30-40 minutes or until the cabbage is tender. Stir occasionally.
Adjust the seasoning if needed.
Once the Hungarian Red Cabbage is cooked to your liking, remove it from the heat.
Serve the cabbage hot as a side dish with traditional Hungarian mains.

This sweet and tangy Hungarian Red Cabbage is a delightful addition to your Hungarian culinary experience, offering vibrant color and robust flavors. Enjoy it alongside dishes like goulash or roasted meats!

Paprika Potatoes

Ingredients:

- 4 large potatoes, peeled and diced
- 1 large onion, finely chopped
- 2 tablespoons vegetable oil or lard
- 2 tablespoons sweet paprika
- 1 teaspoon caraway seeds (optional)
- 1 bell pepper, diced
- 1 tomato, diced
- 2 cloves garlic, minced
- Salt and black pepper to taste
- 1 cup water or vegetable broth
- Chopped fresh parsley for garnish (optional)
- Sour cream for serving (optional)

Instructions:

In a large pot or Dutch oven, heat the vegetable oil or lard over medium heat.
Add the finely chopped onion and sauté until translucent.
Stir in the sweet paprika and caraway seeds (if using) to create a fragrant base for the dish.
Add the diced potatoes to the pot and coat them with the paprika-onion mixture.
Pour in the water or vegetable broth, ensuring it covers the potatoes. Season with salt and black pepper.
Add the diced bell pepper, tomato, and minced garlic to the pot. Stir to combine.
Bring the mixture to a simmer, then reduce the heat to low, cover the pot, and let it cook for approximately 20-25 minutes or until the potatoes are tender. Stir occasionally.
Adjust the seasoning if needed. If you prefer a thicker sauce, you can mash some of the potatoes with a fork and mix them into the liquid.
Once the Paprika Potatoes are cooked, remove the pot from the heat.
Garnish with chopped fresh parsley if desired.
Serve the Paprika Potatoes hot, optionally topped with a dollop of sour cream.

Paprika Potatoes are a comforting and satisfying dish that showcases the distinctive flavors of Hungarian cuisine. Enjoy it as a main course or as a side dish alongside your favorite meats!

Lángos (Fried Bread)

Ingredients:

For the Dough:

- 4 cups all-purpose flour
- 1 teaspoon salt
- 1 teaspoon sugar
- 1 cup lukewarm water
- 1 teaspoon active dry yeast
- 2 tablespoons vegetable oil

For Frying and Toppings:

- Vegetable oil for frying
- Garlic, minced (optional)
- Sour cream
- Grated cheese (e.g., mozzarella or cheddar)
- Chopped fresh parsley (optional)
- Salt

Instructions:

In a small bowl, mix the lukewarm water, sugar, and active dry yeast. Let it sit for about 5-10 minutes until it becomes frothy.
In a large mixing bowl, combine the flour and salt. Make a well in the center.
Pour the yeast mixture and vegetable oil into the well.
Gradually incorporate the flour into the wet ingredients, mixing until a dough forms.
Knead the dough on a floured surface for about 5-7 minutes until it becomes smooth and elastic.
Place the dough back in the bowl, cover it with a kitchen towel, and let it rise in a warm place for 1-2 hours or until it doubles in size.
Punch down the risen dough and divide it into smaller portions.
On a floured surface, roll out each portion into a thin, flat circle.
In a deep fryer or a deep skillet, heat vegetable oil to 350°F (175°C).

Carefully slide the rolled-out dough into the hot oil and fry until golden brown on both sides, about 2-3 minutes per side.

Remove the fried dough (Lángos) from the oil and place it on a paper towel to absorb excess oil.

Optional: Rub the surface of the Lángos with minced garlic while it's still hot.

Top the Lángos with a generous dollop of sour cream, grated cheese, chopped fresh parsley, and a sprinkle of salt.

Serve the Lángos hot and enjoy!

Lángos is best when served immediately, while it's still warm and crispy. It's a versatile dish, and you can get creative with the toppings to suit your preferences.

Krumpli Saláta (Potato Salad)

Ingredients:

- 4 large potatoes, peeled and diced
- 1/2 cup diced carrots
- 1/2 cup frozen peas
- 1/2 cup mayonnaise
- 2 tablespoons sour cream
- 1 tablespoon Dijon mustard
- 1 small red onion, finely chopped
- 2 hard-boiled eggs, chopped
- Salt and black pepper to taste
- Chopped fresh parsley for garnish (optional)

Instructions:

Boil the diced potatoes and carrots in salted water until tender. Add the frozen peas during the last few minutes of cooking. Drain and let them cool.
In a large bowl, combine the mayonnaise, sour cream, and Dijon mustard. Mix well to create the dressing.
Add the cooled potatoes, carrots, and peas to the bowl.
Add the chopped red onion and hard-boiled eggs to the mixture.
Gently fold the ingredients together until everything is well coated with the dressing.
Season the salad with salt and black pepper to taste. Adjust the seasoning as needed.
Refrigerate the Krumpli Saláta for at least 1-2 hours before serving to allow the flavors to meld.
Before serving, garnish with chopped fresh parsley if desired.
Serve the Hungarian Potato Salad chilled as a delightful side dish.

Krumpli Saláta is a refreshing and creamy potato salad with a unique Hungarian twist.

Enjoy it alongside grilled meats, at picnics, or as part of a festive spread.

Desserts:

Dobos Torte

Ingredients:

For the Sponge Cake Layers:

- 6 large eggs, separated
- 1 cup granulated sugar
- 1 cup all-purpose flour
- 1 teaspoon baking powder
- 1/2 cup unsalted butter, melted and cooled

For the Chocolate Buttercream:

- 2 cups unsalted butter, softened
- 1 cup powdered sugar
- 8 ounces dark chocolate, melted and cooled
- 1 teaspoon vanilla extract

For the Caramel Topping:

- 1 cup granulated sugar
- 1/4 cup water
- 2 tablespoons unsalted butter
- 1/2 cup chopped hazelnuts or almonds

Instructions:

1. Preheat the Oven:

- Preheat your oven to 350°F (175°C). Grease and flour a 9-inch (23 cm) round cake pan.

2. Prepare the Sponge Cake Layers:

In a large bowl, beat the egg yolks with sugar until pale and fluffy.
Add melted butter and continue beating.
In a separate bowl, sift together flour and baking powder.

Gradually add the dry ingredients to the egg yolk mixture and mix until well combined.

In another bowl, beat the egg whites until stiff peaks form.

Gently fold the beaten egg whites into the batter until smooth.

Pour the batter into the prepared cake pan and smooth the top.

Bake in the preheated oven for about 20-25 minutes or until a toothpick inserted into the center comes out clean.

Allow the cake layer to cool completely before removing it from the pan.

3. Prepare the Chocolate Buttercream:

In a bowl, beat softened butter until creamy.

Gradually add powdered sugar and continue beating.

Add melted chocolate and vanilla extract, and beat until smooth and fluffy.

Set aside.

4. Assemble the Dobos Torte:

Cut the sponge cake layer into six equal parts.

Place one cake layer on a serving plate and spread a layer of chocolate buttercream on top.

Continue layering cake and buttercream, finishing with a layer of buttercream on top.

5. Prepare the Caramel Topping:

In a saucepan, combine sugar and water. Cook over medium heat without stirring until it turns into a golden caramel.

Remove from heat and add butter, stirring until smooth.

Quickly spread the caramel over the top layer of the cake.

Sprinkle chopped hazelnuts or almonds over the caramel before it sets.

6. Final Touches:

- Allow the caramel to set before slicing and serving.

Dobos Torte is a delightful combination of light sponge cake layers, rich chocolate buttercream, and a crunchy caramel-nut topping, making it a beloved Hungarian dessert.

Hungarian Nut Roll (Diós Beigli)

Ingredients:

For the Dough:

- 4 cups all-purpose flour
- 1 cup unsalted butter, softened
- 1/2 cup granulated sugar
- 1/4 teaspoon salt
- 1 cup milk, lukewarm
- 2 1/4 teaspoons active dry yeast (1 packet)
- 3 large egg yolks

For the Walnut Filling:

- 3 cups ground walnuts
- 1 cup granulated sugar
- 1 cup milk
- 1 teaspoon vanilla extract
- Zest of 1 lemon

For Assembly:

- 1 egg, beaten (for egg wash)
- Powdered sugar (for dusting)

Instructions:

1. Activate the Yeast:

    In a small bowl, combine lukewarm milk and yeast. Let it sit for 5-10 minutes until it becomes frothy.

2. Prepare the Dough:

In a large mixing bowl, cream together softened butter, sugar, and salt.
Add the egg yolks and the activated yeast mixture. Mix well.
Gradually add the flour, kneading until a smooth and elastic dough forms.
Cover the dough and let it rise in a warm place until it doubles in size (approximately 1-2 hours).

3. Make the Walnut Filling:

In a saucepan, combine ground walnuts, sugar, and milk.
Cook over medium heat, stirring continuously until the mixture thickens.
Remove from heat and stir in vanilla extract and lemon zest. Let it cool.

4. Assemble Diós Beigli:

Preheat your oven to 350°F (175°C).
Divide the risen dough into two equal portions.
Roll out each portion into a rectangle on a floured surface.
Spread half of the walnut filling over each rectangle.
Roll up the dough tightly from the long side, forming a log.
Place the rolls on a parchment-lined baking sheet with the seam side down.
Brush the tops with beaten egg for a shiny finish.
Bake in the preheated oven for about 30-35 minutes or until golden brown.

5. Finish and Serve:

Allow the Diós Beigli to cool before slicing.
Dust with powdered sugar before serving.

Enjoy your homemade Hungarian Nut Roll! Diós Beigli is often enjoyed during festive occasions and holidays in Hungary.

Kürtőskalács (Chimney Cake)

Ingredients:

For the Dough:

- 4 cups all-purpose flour
- 1 cup warm milk
- 1/2 cup unsalted butter, melted
- 1/2 cup granulated sugar
- 1 packet (2 1/4 teaspoons) active dry yeast
- 1 teaspoon salt
- 2 large eggs

For Coating:

- 1/2 cup granulated sugar
- 1 teaspoon ground cinnamon (optional)

Instructions:

1. Activate the Yeast:

    In a small bowl, combine warm milk and sugar. Stir until sugar is dissolved. Sprinkle the yeast over the milk mixture and let it sit for 5-10 minutes until it becomes frothy.

2. Prepare the Dough:

    In a large mixing bowl, combine flour and salt.
    Make a well in the center and add the melted butter, activated yeast mixture, and eggs.
    Mix the ingredients until a soft dough forms.
    Knead the dough on a floured surface for about 8-10 minutes until it becomes smooth and elastic.
    Place the dough in a greased bowl, cover it with a kitchen towel, and let it rise in a warm place until it doubles in size (approximately 1-2 hours).

3. Preheat the Oven:

- Preheat your oven to 350°F (175°C). Line a baking sheet with parchment paper.

4. Shape the Kürtőskalács:

    Punch down the risen dough and divide it into equal portions.
    Roll each portion into a long rope, about 1/2 inch thick.
    Combine sugar and ground cinnamon (if using) in a shallow dish.
    Roll each rope in the sugar mixture, coating it evenly.
    Wrap each sugared rope around a Kürtőskalács mold or a cone-shaped object (like a rolling pin) to create the characteristic spiral shape.

5. Bake:

    Place the prepared Kürtőskalács on the parchment-lined baking sheet.
    Bake in the preheated oven for about 20-25 minutes or until golden brown and cooked through.

6. Finish and Serve:

    Allow the Kürtőskalács to cool slightly before removing it from the mold.
    Optionally, dust with more sugar or cinnamon before serving.

Enjoy your homemade Kürtőskalács! This delightful pastry is often enjoyed as a festive treat in Hungary.

Rákóczi Túrós (Cottage Cheese Cake)

Ingredients:

For the Dough:

- 2 1/2 cups all-purpose flour
- 1 cup unsalted butter, cold and diced
- 1/2 cup granulated sugar
- 1 teaspoon baking powder
- 1/4 teaspoon salt
- 2 large egg yolks
- 1/2 cup sour cream

For the Cottage Cheese Filling:

- 2 cups cottage cheese (drained)
- 1 cup granulated sugar
- 3 large eggs
- 1 teaspoon vanilla extract
- Zest of 1 lemon
- 1/4 cup raisins (optional)
- 1/4 cup breadcrumbs (for sprinkling)

For the Topping:

- Powdered sugar (for dusting)

Instructions:

1. Prepare the Dough:

    In a large mixing bowl, combine flour, cold diced butter, sugar, baking powder, and salt.
    Using your fingers or a pastry cutter, work the ingredients together until the mixture resembles breadcrumbs.

Add egg yolks and sour cream to the mixture. Mix until the dough comes together.
Form the dough into a ball, wrap it in plastic wrap, and refrigerate for at least 30 minutes.

2. Preheat the Oven:

- Preheat your oven to 350°F (175°C). Grease a 9-inch (23 cm) springform pan.

3. Roll Out the Dough:

Take the chilled dough and roll it out on a floured surface to fit the bottom and sides of the springform pan.
Press the dough into the bottom and up the sides of the pan. Trim any excess.

4. Prepare the Cottage Cheese Filling:

In a bowl, combine cottage cheese, sugar, eggs, vanilla extract, lemon zest, and raisins (if using). Mix until well combined.
Pour the cottage cheese filling onto the prepared dough in the springform pan.
Sprinkle breadcrumbs evenly over the filling.

5. Bake:

- Bake in the preheated oven for approximately 45-50 minutes or until the top is golden brown and the filling is set.

6. Finish and Serve:

Allow the Rákóczi Túrós to cool in the pan before removing the sides of the springform.
Dust the top with powdered sugar before serving.

Enjoy your homemade Rákóczi Túrós! This cottage cheese cake is a delightful and traditional Hungarian dessert.

Rétes (Strudel) - Apple or Cherry

Ingredients:

For the Strudel Dough:

- 2 1/2 cups all-purpose flour
- 1/2 cup lukewarm water
- 1/2 cup vegetable oil
- 1 large egg
- Pinch of salt

For the Apple Filling:

- 4-5 medium-sized apples, peeled, cored, and thinly sliced
- 1/2 cup granulated sugar
- 1 teaspoon ground cinnamon
- 1/2 cup breadcrumbs
- 1/2 cup chopped walnuts or almonds
- 1/4 cup raisins (optional)

For the Cherry Filling:

- 2 cups pitted cherries (fresh or frozen)
- 1/2 cup granulated sugar
- 1 tablespoon cornstarch
- 1/2 teaspoon almond extract (optional)

For Assembly:

- Melted butter for brushing
- Powdered sugar for dusting

Instructions:

1. Prepare the Strudel Dough:

In a large bowl, combine flour, lukewarm water, vegetable oil, egg, and a pinch of salt.
Mix the ingredients until a dough forms. Knead the dough on a floured surface until it becomes smooth.
Place the dough in a bowl, cover it with a kitchen towel, and let it rest for about 1 hour.

2. Prepare the Fillings:

For the Apple Filling:

In a bowl, combine sliced apples, granulated sugar, ground cinnamon, breadcrumbs, chopped nuts, and raisins (if using). Mix well.

For the Cherry Filling:

In a saucepan, combine pitted cherries, granulated sugar, cornstarch, and almond extract (if using). Cook over medium heat until the mixture thickens. Let it cool.

3. Roll Out the Dough:

Preheat your oven to 350°F (175°C).
On a floured surface, roll out the rested dough into a thin rectangle.

4. Assemble the Rétes:

Brush the rolled-out dough with melted butter.
Spread the prepared filling (either apple or cherry) evenly over the dough, leaving some space at the edges.
Carefully roll the dough with the filling into a log, sealing the edges.

5. Bake:

Place the rolled Rétes on a parchment-lined baking sheet.
Bake in the preheated oven for about 30-35 minutes or until golden brown.

6. Finish and Serve:

Allow the Rétes to cool slightly before slicing.
Dust with powdered sugar before serving.

Enjoy your homemade Rétes with either Apple or Cherry filling! This traditional Hungarian strudel is perfect for dessert or a sweet treat with coffee or tea.

Somlói Galuska (Chocolate Sponge Cake)

Ingredients:

For the Chocolate Sponge Cake:

- 6 large eggs, separated
- 1 cup granulated sugar
- 1 cup all-purpose flour
- 2 tablespoons cocoa powder
- 1 teaspoon baking powder
- 1/4 teaspoon salt

For the Pastry Cream:

- 2 cups whole milk
- 1/2 cup granulated sugar
- 1/4 cup cornstarch
- 4 large egg yolks
- 1 teaspoon vanilla extract

For the Chocolate Sauce:

- 1 cup dark chocolate, chopped
- 1/2 cup heavy cream
- 2 tablespoons unsalted butter

For Assembly:

- 1 cup ground walnuts or hazelnuts
- Whipped cream (optional)
- Chocolate shavings (for garnish)

Instructions:

1. Prepare the Chocolate Sponge Cake:

    Preheat your oven to 350°F (175°C). Grease and flour a 9x13-inch baking dish.
    In a bowl, sift together flour, cocoa powder, baking powder, and salt.
    In a separate bowl, beat egg yolks with sugar until pale and fluffy.

Gradually add the dry ingredients to the egg yolk mixture, mixing until well combined.
In another bowl, beat egg whites until stiff peaks form.
Gently fold the beaten egg whites into the batter until smooth.
Pour the batter into the prepared baking dish and smooth the top.
Bake for 20-25 minutes or until a toothpick inserted into the center comes out clean.
Allow the chocolate sponge cake to cool completely.

2. Prepare the Pastry Cream:

In a saucepan, heat milk until just simmering.
In a bowl, whisk together sugar, cornstarch, and egg yolks until well combined.
Slowly pour the hot milk into the egg mixture, whisking constantly.
Return the mixture to the saucepan and cook over medium heat, stirring constantly, until it thickens.
Remove from heat, stir in vanilla extract, and let it cool.

3. Prepare the Chocolate Sauce:

In a heatproof bowl, combine chopped dark chocolate, heavy cream, and butter. Place the bowl over a pot of simmering water (double boiler) and stir until the chocolate and butter melt and the mixture is smooth. Remove from heat and let it cool.

4. Assemble Somlói Galuska:

Cut the cooled chocolate sponge cake into squares.
In serving glasses or a trifle dish, layer the chocolate sponge cake squares, pastry cream, chocolate sauce, and ground nuts.
Repeat the layers until all ingredients are used, finishing with a layer of chocolate sauce and a sprinkle of ground nuts.
Refrigerate for a few hours or overnight to allow the flavors to meld.

5. Finish and Serve:

Before serving, garnish with whipped cream and chocolate shavings if desired.

Enjoy your homemade Somlói Galuska! This indulgent Hungarian dessert is sure to delight chocolate lovers with its rich layers and textures.

Gesztenyepüré (Chestnut Puree)

Ingredients:

- 2 cups cooked and peeled chestnuts (fresh or vacuum-packed)
- 1 cup milk
- 1/2 cup granulated sugar (adjust to taste)
- 1 teaspoon vanilla extract
- Pinch of salt
- Whipped cream (for serving, optional)

Instructions:

1. Cook and Peel the Chestnuts:

- If using fresh chestnuts, make a small cut on the flat side of each chestnut, then roast or boil them until tender. Peel the chestnuts while they are still warm.

2. Make the Chestnut Puree:

In a blender or food processor, combine the cooked and peeled chestnuts, milk, sugar, vanilla extract, and a pinch of salt.
Blend the mixture until smooth and creamy.

3. Adjust Sweetness:

- Taste the chestnut puree and adjust the sweetness by adding more sugar if needed. Blend again to combine.

4. Serve:

- Transfer the chestnut puree to serving bowls or glasses.

5. Optional: Garnish with Whipped Cream:

- If desired, top each serving with a dollop of whipped cream.

6. Chill (Optional):

- You can serve the Gesztenyepüré immediately at room temperature, or refrigerate it for a few hours for a chilled dessert.

7. Finish and Enjoy:

- Before serving, you can garnish the Gesztenyepüré with additional chestnut pieces or a sprinkle of powdered sugar if desired.

Enjoy your homemade Gesztenyepüré! This creamy chestnut puree is a delightful and comforting dessert that captures the unique flavor of chestnuts.

Pastries and Breads:

Pogácsa (Cheese Biscuits)

Ingredients:

- 2 1/2 cups all-purpose flour
- 1 cup unsalted butter, cold and diced
- 1 1/4 cups grated cheese (a combination of sharp cheddar and parmesan works well)
- 1 teaspoon salt
- 1 teaspoon baking powder
- 1/2 cup sour cream
- 1 large egg for the dough, plus 1 egg for egg wash
- Optional: caraway seeds, sesame seeds, or paprika for topping

Instructions:

1. Preheat Oven:

- Preheat your oven to 375°F (190°C). Line a baking sheet with parchment paper.

2. Prepare the Dough:

In a large mixing bowl, combine the flour, salt, and baking powder.
Add the cold, diced butter to the flour mixture and cut it in using a pastry cutter or your fingers until the mixture resembles coarse crumbs.
Stir in the grated cheese.
In a small bowl, whisk together the sour cream and one egg.
Add the sour cream mixture to the flour mixture and stir until a soft dough forms.

3. Shape the Pogácsa:

Turn the dough out onto a floured surface and knead it gently a few times.
Roll out the dough to about 1/2 inch thickness.
Use a round cookie cutter or a glass to cut out individual pogácsa rounds.

4. Egg Wash and Toppings:

Beat the remaining egg in a small bowl to create an egg wash.

Brush the tops of each pogácsa round with the egg wash.
Optional: Sprinkle caraway seeds, sesame seeds, or paprika on top for added flavor and decoration.

5. Bake:

- Place the pogácsa rounds on the prepared baking sheet and bake in the preheated oven for 15-20 minutes or until they are golden brown.

6. Cool and Serve:

- Allow the pogácsa to cool slightly before serving. They can be enjoyed warm or at room temperature.

These Cheese Pogácsa are perfect for serving at gatherings or enjoying as a snack with a cup of tea. Feel free to experiment with different types of cheese or add herbs for variations in flavor.

Kifli (Nut or Poppy Seed Crescent Rolls)

Ingredients:

For the Dough:

- 4 cups all-purpose flour
- 1 cup unsalted butter, softened
- 1/2 cup sour cream
- 3 egg yolks
- 1/2 cup granulated sugar
- 1 package (2 1/4 teaspoons) active dry yeast
- 1/2 cup warm milk
- 1/4 teaspoon salt

For the Filling (choose either Nut or Poppy Seed):

Nut Filling:

- 1 1/2 cups ground walnuts or hazelnuts
- 1/2 cup sugar
- 1/2 cup milk

Poppy Seed Filling:

- 1 1/2 cups poppy seeds
- 1/2 cup sugar
- 1/2 cup milk
- 1 tablespoon unsalted butter

For Assembly and Topping:

- Additional melted butter for brushing
- Powdered sugar for dusting

Instructions:

1. Prepare the Dough:

   In a small bowl, dissolve the yeast in warm milk with a pinch of sugar. Let it sit until it becomes frothy.
   In a large mixing bowl, cream together the softened butter and sugar until light and fluffy.
   Add the egg yolks and sour cream to the butter mixture and mix well.
   Stir in the activated yeast mixture.
   Gradually add the flour and salt to form a soft dough.
   Knead the dough on a floured surface until smooth.
   Divide the dough into four equal parts, shape them into balls, and refrigerate for at least 1 hour.

2. Prepare the Filling:

Nut Filling:

   In a saucepan, combine ground nuts, sugar, and milk.
   Cook over medium heat, stirring continuously until the mixture thickens.
   Let the nut filling cool.

Poppy Seed Filling:

   In a saucepan, combine poppy seeds, sugar, milk, and butter.
   Cook over medium heat, stirring continuously until the mixture thickens.
   Let the poppy seed filling cool.

3. Assemble and Shape Kifli:

   Preheat your oven to 350°F (175°C). Line baking sheets with parchment paper.
   Take one portion of the chilled dough and roll it out into a thin circle on a floured surface.
   Spread a thin layer of the chosen filling (nut or poppy seed) over the dough.
   Using a pizza cutter or a knife, cut the circle into eight wedges.
   Roll each wedge from the wider end to form a crescent shape.
   Place the crescents on the prepared baking sheets.

4. Bake:

- Bake in the preheated oven for about 15-20 minutes or until the Kifli are golden brown.

5. Finish and Serve:

While still warm, brush the baked Kifli with melted butter.
Dust with powdered sugar before serving.

Enjoy your homemade Nut or Poppy Seed Crescent Rolls (Kifli)! These delightful pastries are a perfect treat for special occasions or holiday celebrations.

Zsemle (Soft White Rolls)

Ingredients:

- 4 cups all-purpose flour
- 1 tablespoon sugar
- 1 teaspoon salt
- 1 tablespoon active dry yeast
- 1 1/2 cups warm milk
- 1/4 cup vegetable oil or melted butter
- 1 egg (for the dough)
- Sesame seeds or poppy seeds for topping (optional)

Instructions:

1. Activate the Yeast:

    In a small bowl, combine the warm milk, sugar, and active dry yeast. Let it sit for about 5-10 minutes until the mixture becomes frothy.

2. Prepare the Dough:

    In a large mixing bowl, combine the flour and salt.
    Add the activated yeast mixture, vegetable oil (or melted butter), and one beaten egg to the flour mixture.
    Mix the ingredients until a dough forms.

3. Knead the Dough:

    Turn the dough out onto a floured surface and knead it for about 8-10 minutes until it becomes smooth and elastic.

4. First Rise:

    Place the kneaded dough in a greased bowl, cover it with a clean kitchen towel, and let it rise in a warm place for about 1-1.5 hours or until it doubles in size.

5. Shape the Rolls:

    Punch down the risen dough and divide it into equal portions to form rolls. Shape each portion into a round roll and place them on a baking sheet lined with parchment paper.

6. Second Rise:

    Cover the formed rolls with a kitchen towel and let them rise for an additional 30-45 minutes.

7. Preheat the Oven:

    - Preheat your oven to 375°F (190°C).

8. Egg Wash and Topping:

    Beat an egg and brush the tops of the risen rolls with the egg wash. Optionally, sprinkle sesame seeds or poppy seeds on top for added texture.

9. Bake:

    - Bake in the preheated oven for 15-20 minutes or until the Zsemle are golden brown and sound hollow when tapped.

10. Cool and Serve:

    Allow the Zsemle to cool on a wire rack before serving.

Enjoy your homemade Zsemle! These soft white rolls are perfect for sandwiches, breakfast, or as a side dish with soups and stews.

Lángos (Deep-Fried Flatbread)

Ingredients:

For the Dough:

- 4 cups all-purpose flour
- 1 teaspoon salt
- 1 teaspoon sugar
- 1 cup warm water
- 1 teaspoon active dry yeast
- 2 tablespoons vegetable oil

For Frying:

- Vegetable oil for deep frying

Toppings (Optional):

- Garlic, minced
- Sour cream
- Grated cheese (like mozzarella)
- Salt
- Paprika

Instructions:

1. Activate the Yeast:

    In a small bowl, combine warm water, sugar, and active dry yeast. Let it sit for about 5-10 minutes until frothy.

2. Prepare the Dough:

    In a large mixing bowl, combine the flour and salt.
    Add the activated yeast mixture and vegetable oil to the flour.

Mix the ingredients to form a dough.
Knead the dough on a floured surface until it becomes smooth.

3. First Rise:

   Place the kneaded dough in a greased bowl, cover it with a clean kitchen towel, and let it rise in a warm place for about 1-1.5 hours or until it doubles in size.

4. Shape the Lángos:

   Punch down the risen dough and divide it into smaller portions.
   Roll each portion into a flat, round shape.

5. Deep Frying:

   Heat vegetable oil in a deep fryer or a large, deep pan to around 350°F (175°C).
   Carefully place the flattened dough into the hot oil and fry until both sides are golden brown.
   Use a slotted spoon to remove the Lángos from the oil and place them on a paper towel to drain excess oil.

6. Serve with Toppings:

   While still warm, you can brush the Lángos with minced garlic, spread sour cream, sprinkle grated cheese, salt, and paprika, or customize with your favorite toppings.

7. Enjoy:

   - Serve the Lángos immediately while they are still warm and crispy.

Lángos is a versatile dish, and you can experiment with different toppings to suit your taste. It's a delicious and comforting street food that is perfect for a snack or a casual meal.

Diós Kalács (Walnut Bread)

Ingredients:

For the Dough:

- 4 cups all-purpose flour
- 1/2 cup sugar
- 1 teaspoon salt
- 1 packet (2 1/4 teaspoons) active dry yeast
- 1 cup warm milk
- 1/2 cup unsalted butter, melted
- 3 large eggs

For the Filling:

- 1 1/2 cups finely chopped walnuts
- 1/2 cup sugar
- 1 teaspoon ground cinnamon
- 2 tablespoons unsalted butter, melted

For the Glaze:

- 1/2 cup powdered sugar
- 1-2 tablespoons milk
- 1/2 teaspoon vanilla extract

Instructions:

1. Activate the Yeast:

    In a small bowl, combine warm milk and a teaspoon of sugar. Sprinkle the yeast over the milk, stir gently, and let it sit for about 5-10 minutes until frothy.

2. Prepare the Dough:

    In a large mixing bowl, combine flour, sugar, and salt.
    In a separate bowl, whisk together the activated yeast, melted butter, and eggs.
    Pour the wet ingredients into the dry ingredients and mix to form a dough.
    Knead the dough on a floured surface until it becomes smooth and elastic.

3. First Rise:

   Place the dough in a greased bowl, cover it with a clean kitchen towel, and let it rise in a warm place for about 1-1.5 hours or until it doubles in size.

4. Prepare the Filling:

   In a bowl, mix together the finely chopped walnuts, sugar, cinnamon, and melted butter to create the filling.

5. Shape the Kalács:

   Punch down the risen dough and divide it in half.
   Roll out one portion into a rectangle on a floured surface.
   Spread half of the walnut filling evenly over the rolled-out dough.
   Roll the dough into a log, sealing the edges.
   Repeat the process with the second half of the dough and filling.

6. Second Rise:

   Place the rolled walnut-filled dough logs on a baking sheet lined with parchment paper.
   Cover them with a kitchen towel and let them rise for an additional 30-45 minutes.

7. Bake:

   Preheat your oven to 350°F (175°C).
   Bake the Kalács in the preheated oven for about 25-30 minutes or until they are golden brown.

8. Prepare the Glaze:

   In a small bowl, whisk together powdered sugar, milk, and vanilla extract to create the glaze.

9. Finish:

   Once the Kalács are baked and still warm, drizzle the glaze over the top.
   Allow the bread to cool before slicing and serving.

Enjoy your homemade Diós Kalács! This walnut-filled bread is a delightful treat with a sweet and nutty flavor.

Drinks:

Pálinka (Fruit Brandy)

Ingredients:

- 10-15 kg of ripe fruits (plums, apricots, cherries, pears, or apples are commonly used)
- Water
- Sugar (optional)
- Yeast (optional)

Equipment:

- Fermentation vessel with airlock
- Distillation apparatus (pot still or alembic)
- Glass containers for collecting and storing the distilled spirit

Instructions:

1. Fruit Preparation:

- Wash and remove any stems or pits from the fruits. Cut them into small pieces or crush them to extract juice.

2. Fermentation:

Place the fruit mash in a fermentation vessel.
If the natural sugar content is low, you can add sugar to increase alcohol production. This step is optional, as some traditional Pálinka recipes rely solely on the fruit's natural sugars.
Optionally, you can add a small amount of yeast to kickstart fermentation. However, many traditional recipes rely on wild yeast present on the fruit.

3. Fermentation Process:

Cover the fermentation vessel with an airlock to allow gases to escape while preventing contaminants from entering.
Allow the fruit mash to ferment for a few weeks until the bubbling subsides, indicating the end of fermentation.

4. Distillation:

   Transfer the fermented fruit mash to the distillation apparatus.
   Heat the mash slowly, and collect the distilled spirit in separate containers.
   Discard the initial portion, known as the "heads," as it may contain impurities.
   Collect the "heart" portion, which is the desirable spirit with a balanced flavor profile.
   Stop collecting before reaching the "tails," as this portion may contain undesirable compounds.

5. Aging (Optional):

   - Some Pálinka varieties are aged in wooden barrels to enhance their flavors. This step is optional and depends on personal preference.

6. Bottling:

   - Once distilled and, if applicable, aged, transfer the Pálinka to glass containers for storage. It is typically enjoyed at a high proof and may be diluted with water before consumption.

Important Notes:

- Making distilled spirits at home may be subject to legal restrictions in some regions. Ensure you comply with local regulations.
- Distillation should be performed with care and attention to safety, as it involves the use of heat and potentially flammable materials.

This simplified recipe provides an overview of the basic steps involved in making Pálinka. If you're new to distillation, it's recommended to seek guidance or consult with experienced individuals to ensure a safe and successful process.

Unicum (Herbal Liqueur)

Ingredients:

- 1 bottle (750 ml) of neutral grain spirit (vodka or grain alcohol)
- Assorted dried herbs and spices (such as gentian root, angelica root, juniper berries, cinnamon, cloves, and citrus peel)
- 1 tablespoon honey
- Water
- Optional: additional herbs or spices to adjust the flavor

Instructions:

1. Herb Infusion:

    Combine the dried herbs and spices in a large, sealable glass jar.
    Pour the neutral grain spirit over the herbs and spices, ensuring they are fully submerged.
    Seal the jar and let the mixture steep in a cool, dark place for several weeks.
    Shake the jar occasionally to agitate the ingredients.

2. Straining:

    After the infusion period, strain the liquid through a fine mesh strainer or cheesecloth to remove the solid particles.
    Press down on the herbs to extract as much flavor as possible.

3. Sweetening:

    Dissolve honey in a small amount of warm water to create a honey syrup.
    Add the honey syrup to the infused liquid and mix well. Adjust the sweetness to your liking.

4. Dilution:

    Taste the liqueur and determine if it needs further dilution. If so, add water gradually until you reach the desired strength.

5. Adjusting Flavor (Optional):

If the flavor needs adjustment, you can add additional herbs or spices in small increments until you achieve the desired balance.

6. Aging (Optional):

    Allow the liqueur to age in a sealed container for a few weeks to allow the flavors to meld and mellow.

7. Bottling:

    Once you are satisfied with the flavor, strain the liqueur once more and bottle it in a clean, airtight container.

Keep in mind that this simplified version is inspired by the general characteristics of Unicum and may not replicate the exact taste of the commercial product. The original recipe is a closely guarded secret, and Unicum enthusiasts appreciate its unique and authentic flavor.

Fröccs (Wine Spritzer)

Ingredients:

- White or red wine of your choice (dry wines work well)
- Soda water or sparkling mineral water
- Ice cubes (optional)
- Lemon or lime wedges for garnish (optional)

Instructions:

1. Choose the Wine:

- Select a white or red wine based on your preference. Dry wines are commonly used for Fröccs.

2. Choose the Soda Water:

- Use soda water or sparkling mineral water for the spritzer. The effervescence adds a refreshing quality.

3. Choose the Ratio:

- The ratio of wine to soda water can vary depending on personal taste. A common ratio is 1:1, but you can adjust it to make the drink lighter or stronger.

4. Prepare the Fröccs:

    Fill a glass with ice cubes if desired.
    Pour the desired amount of wine into the glass.
    Top up the glass with soda water or sparkling mineral water.

5. Mix Gently:

- Gently stir the mixture to combine the wine and soda water. Be careful not to lose the carbonation.

6. Garnish (Optional):

- Garnish the Fröccs with lemon or lime wedges for a citrusy twist.

7. Serve:

- Serve the Fröccs chilled and enjoy it on a hot day or as a light and refreshing beverage.

Fröccs Variations:

- Kisfröccs (Small Spritzer): A lighter version with more soda water.
- Nagyfröccs (Large Spritzer): A stronger version with less soda water.
- Spritzer with Aperitif: Some variations include adding aperitifs or liqueurs for extra flavor.

Fröccs is a versatile and social drink, often enjoyed in outdoor settings, picnics, and gatherings. It's a simple yet delightful way to enjoy wine in a refreshing format.

Palinka Sour

Ingredients:

- 2 oz pálinka (traditional Hungarian fruit brandy)
- 3/4 oz fresh lemon juice
- 1/2 oz simple syrup
- Ice cubes
- Lemon wheel or twist for garnish

For Simple Syrup:

- 1 part water
- 1 part sugar

Instructions:

1. Prepare Simple Syrup (if not available):

    In a small saucepan, combine equal parts water and sugar.
    Heat over medium heat, stirring until the sugar dissolves.
    Allow it to cool before using. Extra syrup can be stored in the refrigerator.

2. Mix the Pálinka Sour:

    In a cocktail shaker, combine pálinka, fresh lemon juice, and simple syrup.
    Add ice cubes to the shaker.
    Shake the ingredients well to chill the mixture.

3. Strain and Serve:

    Strain the cocktail into a rocks glass filled with ice.
    Alternatively, you can serve it neat in a chilled glass without ice.

4. Garnish:

    - Garnish the Pálinka Sour with a lemon wheel or twist.

5. Enjoy:

- Sip and savor the delightful combination of pálinka's fruity notes, lemony freshness, and a touch of sweetness.

Feel free to adjust the proportions of lemon juice and simple syrup to suit your taste preferences. Some variations might include experimenting with different types of pálinka or adding a dash of bitters for extra complexity.

Remember to drink responsibly, and enjoy the unique flavors of this Hungarian-inspired cocktail!

Snacks:

Tökmag (Roasted Pumpkin Seeds)

Ingredients:

- Fresh pumpkin seeds
- Olive oil or melted butter
- Salt, to taste
- Optional seasonings: garlic powder, paprika, cayenne pepper, or your favorite spices

Instructions:

1. Harvesting Pumpkin Seeds:

- When you carve a pumpkin, scoop out the seeds from the pumpkin's interior.

2. Cleaning and Separating:

Rinse the pumpkin seeds thoroughly under cold water to remove any pumpkin pulp.
Use your fingers to separate the seeds from any remaining pumpkin strands.

3. Boiling (Optional):

- Some people like to boil the pumpkin seeds in salted water for about 10 minutes before roasting. This can enhance their flavor and make them easier to digest.

4. Preparing for Roasting:

Preheat your oven to 300°F (150°C).
Pat the cleaned and dried pumpkin seeds with a paper towel to remove excess moisture.

5. Seasoning:

In a bowl, toss the pumpkin seeds with a small amount of olive oil or melted butter.
Add salt to taste and any optional seasonings you desire, such as garlic powder, paprika, or cayenne pepper. Mix well to coat the seeds evenly.

6. Roasting:

Spread the seasoned pumpkin seeds in a single layer on a baking sheet.
Roast in the preheated oven for about 20-30 minutes or until the seeds are golden brown and crispy. Stir or shake the pan occasionally for even roasting.

7. Cooling:

- Allow the roasted pumpkin seeds to cool before enjoying.

8. Store:

- Once completely cooled, store the roasted pumpkin seeds in an airtight container. They can be kept for several weeks.

Variations:

- Sweet Pumpkin Seeds: Toss the seeds with cinnamon and sugar before roasting for a sweet variation.
- Savory Pumpkin Seeds: Experiment with different savory seasonings such as onion powder, cumin, or chili powder.

Roasted pumpkin seeds are a nutritious and crunchy snack, rich in protein, fiber, and various vitamins and minerals. Enjoy them on their own, sprinkle them on salads, or use them as a topping for soups!

Túrós Rudi (Chocolate-Covered Cottage Cheese Bars)

Ingredients:

For the Filling:

- 1 cup cottage cheese (drained to remove excess liquid)
- 2 tablespoons powdered sugar
- 1 teaspoon vanilla extract
- Zest of 1 lemon (optional)
- Fruit jam (apricot or strawberry, optional)

For the Chocolate Coating:

- 200 grams dark chocolate (70% cocoa or your preference)
- 1-2 tablespoons vegetable oil

Instructions:

1. Prepare the Filling:

    In a bowl, combine the drained cottage cheese, powdered sugar, vanilla extract, and lemon zest (if using). Mix well until smooth and creamy.
    Optionally, spread a thin layer of fruit jam on a flat surface or a silicone mold to create a fruity layer in the middle of the bars.

2. Shape the Filling:

    Divide the cottage cheese mixture into small, rectangular shapes or use the fruit jam as a middle layer to create bars.

3. Freeze the Filling:

    Place the shaped bars in the freezer for about 1-2 hours to firm up.

4. Prepare the Chocolate Coating:

    In a heatproof bowl, melt the dark chocolate using a double boiler or in the microwave at 30-second intervals. Stir in between intervals.

Once melted, add vegetable oil to the chocolate and stir until smooth. The oil helps create a glossy finish on the chocolate coating.

5. Coat the Bars:

   Remove the frozen cottage cheese bars from the freezer.
   Using a fork or toothpick, dip each bar into the melted chocolate, coating it completely.
   Place the coated bars on a parchment paper-lined tray.

6. Set and Enjoy:

   Allow the chocolate-coated bars to set in the refrigerator for at least 30 minutes or until the chocolate hardens.
   Once set, Túrós Rudi is ready to be enjoyed!

These homemade Túrós Rudi bars offer a delightful contrast between the creamy cottage cheese filling and the rich chocolate coating. Adjust the sweetness to your liking and experiment with different fruit jam flavors for added variety. Enjoy this classic Hungarian treat!

Pogácsa (Savory Scones)

Ingredients:

- 3 1/2 cups all-purpose flour
- 1 cup unsalted butter, cold and cut into small pieces
- 1 cup sour cream
- 1 teaspoon salt
- 1 teaspoon baking powder
- 1/2 teaspoon baking soda
- 1 1/2 cups grated cheese (commonly used: a combination of aged Gouda and Parmesan)
- 1 egg (for egg wash)
- Sesame seeds or caraway seeds for topping (optional)

Instructions:

1. Preheat the Oven:

- Preheat your oven to 375°F (190°C).

2. Mix Dry Ingredients:

In a large mixing bowl, combine the flour, salt, baking powder, and baking soda. Add the cold, diced butter to the flour mixture.

3. Incorporate Butter:

- Use your fingertips or a pastry cutter to work the butter into the flour until the mixture resembles coarse crumbs.

4. Add Sour Cream and Cheese:

Stir in the sour cream until the dough starts coming together.
Add the grated cheese and knead the dough until it forms a smooth, cohesive ball.

5. Roll and Cut:

Roll out the dough on a floured surface to about 1/2 inch (1.3 cm) thickness.

Use a round cookie cutter or a glass to cut out individual pogácsa.

6. Arrange on Baking Sheet:

- Place the cut pogácsa on a baking sheet lined with parchment paper.

7. Egg Wash:

In a small bowl, beat the egg to create an egg wash.
Brush the tops of the pogácsa with the egg wash.

8. Optional Toppings:

- Sprinkle sesame seeds or caraway seeds on top of each pogácsa if desired.

9. Bake:

- Bake in the preheated oven for approximately 20-25 minutes or until the pogácsa are golden brown.

10. Cool and Enjoy:

- Allow the pogácsa to cool slightly before serving. They can be enjoyed warm or at room temperature.

Variations:

- Ham and Cheese Pogácsa: Add diced ham along with the cheese to create a heartier version.
- Herb Pogácsa: Mix in fresh or dried herbs such as thyme, rosemary, or chives for added flavor.
- Spicy Pogácsa: Incorporate a pinch of cayenne pepper or paprika for a kick of heat.

Pogácsa is a versatile snack and can be enjoyed with various fillings and flavors. It's a classic Hungarian treat often served during gatherings, celebrations, or as an accompaniment to soups.

Túró Rudi Mousse

Ingredients:

- 1 cup cottage cheese (túró)
- 1 cup Greek yogurt
- 1/2 cup powdered sugar (adjust to taste)
- 1 teaspoon vanilla extract
- 1 cup heavy cream
- 200 grams dark chocolate, melted and cooled
- Chocolate shavings or grated chocolate for garnish (optional)

Instructions:

1. Prepare the Túró Mixture:

    In a blender or food processor, combine the cottage cheese, Greek yogurt, powdered sugar, and vanilla extract.
    Blend until the mixture is smooth and well combined.

2. Whip the Heavy Cream:

    In a separate bowl, whip the heavy cream until stiff peaks form.
    Gently fold the whipped cream into the túró mixture until well incorporated.

3. Add Melted Chocolate:

    Pour the melted and cooled dark chocolate into the túró mixture.
    Gently fold the chocolate into the mixture until smooth and uniform.

4. Chill:

    - Transfer the Túró Rudi Mousse into serving glasses or bowls.
    - Chill in the refrigerator for at least 2-3 hours to allow the mousse to set.

5. Garnish (Optional):

    - Before serving, garnish the mousse with chocolate shavings or grated chocolate if desired.

6. Serve and Enjoy:

- Serve the Túró Rudi Mousse chilled and enjoy the creamy, chocolatey goodness.

This Túró Rudi Mousse offers a delightful twist on the classic Hungarian sweet, combining the richness of chocolate with the light and airy texture of the mousse. It makes for a perfect treat for special occasions or as a decadent dessert for any day.

Breakfast:

Rakott Krumpli (Layered Potatoes with Eggs)

Ingredients:

- 4-5 large potatoes, peeled and thinly sliced
- 6 hard-boiled eggs, peeled and sliced
- 1 large onion, finely chopped
- 2 tablespoons vegetable oil
- 2 tablespoons sweet Hungarian paprika
- Salt and pepper to taste
- 2 cups sour cream
- 1 cup grated cheese (commonly used: Emmental or Gouda)
- Butter for greasing the baking dish
- Fresh parsley for garnish (optional)

Instructions:

1. Preheat the Oven:

- Preheat your oven to 375°F (190°C).

2. Prepare Potatoes:

- Peel and thinly slice the potatoes.

3. Sauté Onions:

   In a pan, heat the vegetable oil over medium heat.
   Add chopped onions and sauté until they become translucent.

4. Add Paprika:

- Stir in the sweet Hungarian paprika, cooking briefly to release its flavor. Be careful not to burn the paprika.

5. Mix with Sour Cream:

- Remove the pan from heat and mix in the sour cream. Season with salt and pepper to taste. This creates the paprika-infused sour cream sauce.

6. Grease Baking Dish:

- Grease a baking dish with butter.

7. Assemble Layers:

Place a layer of sliced potatoes at the bottom of the baking dish.
Add a layer of sliced hard-boiled eggs.
Pour a portion of the paprika-infused sour cream sauce over the layers.
Repeat the layers until all ingredients are used, finishing with a layer of sour cream sauce on top.

8. Top with Grated Cheese:

- Sprinkle the grated cheese over the top layer.

9. Bake:

- Bake in the preheated oven for about 40-50 minutes or until the potatoes are tender and the top is golden brown.

10. Garnish and Serve:

- If desired, garnish with fresh parsley before serving.

Rakott Krumpli is a comforting and hearty dish that highlights the delicious combination of potatoes, eggs, and the rich paprika sour cream sauce. It's often served as a main course or a side dish in Hungarian cuisine. Enjoy the layers of flavor in this classic dish!

Hungarian Omelette

Ingredients:

- 4 large eggs
- 1 onion, finely chopped
- 1 red bell pepper, diced
- 1 green bell pepper, diced
- 2 tomatoes, diced
- 2 tablespoons vegetable oil
- 1 teaspoon sweet Hungarian paprika
- Salt and pepper to taste
- Fresh parsley, chopped (for garnish, optional)

Instructions:

1. Sauté Vegetables:

    Heat vegetable oil in a pan over medium heat.
    Add chopped onions and sauté until they become translucent.
    Add diced red and green bell peppers, and continue to sauté until the peppers are softened.

2. Add Tomatoes and Paprika:

    - Add the diced tomatoes to the pan and stir in the sweet Hungarian paprika. Cook until the tomatoes break down and the mixture becomes slightly saucy.

3. Season:

    - Season the vegetable mixture with salt and pepper to taste.

4. Beat Eggs:

    - In a bowl, beat the eggs until well combined.

5. Pour Eggs Over Vegetables:

    - Pour the beaten eggs over the sautéed vegetables. Allow the eggs to set slightly around the edges.

6. Stir and Cook:

- Gently stir the eggs and vegetables together, allowing the eggs to cook through. Continue cooking until the eggs are set but still moist.

7. Garnish and Serve:

- Garnish the Hungarian omelette with fresh parsley if desired.

8. Serve Warm:

- Serve the omelette warm, either on its own or with crusty bread.

Variations:

- Cheese: Add grated cheese (such as Hungarian Trappista or another mild cheese) for a creamy variation.
- Spices: Experiment with additional spices like cumin or smoked paprika for extra flavor.

This Hungarian-style omelette is a quick and flavorful dish that captures the essence of Hungarian cuisine. It's a perfect breakfast or brunch option, and the combination of peppers, tomatoes, and paprika provides a unique and delicious taste. Enjoy!

Túróscsusza (Noodles with Curd)

Ingredients:

- 250g egg noodles (csusza or wide egg noodles)
- 200g túró (Hungarian curd cheese)
- 2 tablespoons butter
- 2-3 tablespoons powdered sugar (adjust to taste)
- 1 teaspoon vanilla sugar or vanilla extract
- Pinch of salt
- Optional toppings: cinnamon, raisins, or grated lemon zest

Instructions:

1. Cook Egg Noodles:

- Cook the egg noodles according to the package instructions. Drain and set aside.

2. Prepare Túró Mixture:

In a bowl, mix the túró (curd cheese) with powdered sugar, vanilla sugar or vanilla extract, and a pinch of salt.
Adjust the sweetness to your liking by adding more or less powdered sugar.

3. Combine with Egg Noodles:

- Add the cooked and drained egg noodles to the túró mixture. Mix well to combine.

4. Sauté in Butter:

In a pan, melt the butter over medium heat.
Add the túró and noodle mixture to the pan and sauté briefly, allowing the flavors to meld. Stir gently to avoid breaking the noodles.

5. Optional Toppings:

- Add optional toppings such as a sprinkle of cinnamon, raisins, or grated lemon zest for extra flavor.

6. Serve Warm:

- Serve Túróscsusza warm, either as is or with your preferred toppings.

Túróscsusza is a versatile dish, and its sweetness can be adjusted to suit individual preferences. It's a comforting and simple dessert that highlights the creamy texture of túró combined with the softness of egg noodles. Enjoy this Hungarian treat for a delightful and satisfying experience!

Holiday Specialties:

Beigli (Christmas Poppy Seed and Walnut Roll)

Ingredients:

For the Dough:

- 4 cups all-purpose flour
- 1 cup unsalted butter, softened
- 1 cup granulated sugar
- 3 large eggs
- 1 package (1/4 ounce) active dry yeast
- 1 cup sour cream
- 1/4 teaspoon salt

For the Poppy Seed Filling:

- 1 1/2 cups ground poppy seeds
- 1 cup milk
- 1 cup granulated sugar
- 1 tablespoon honey
- 1 tablespoon unsalted butter
- Zest of 1 lemon

For the Walnut Filling:

- 2 cups ground walnuts
- 1 cup milk
- 1 cup granulated sugar
- 1 tablespoon honey
- 1 tablespoon unsalted butter
- Zest of 1 orange

For Assembly:

- 1 egg (for egg wash)
- Powdered sugar (for dusting)

Instructions:

1. Prepare the Dough:

   Dissolve the yeast in a small amount of warm milk with a pinch of sugar. Let it sit until it becomes frothy.
   In a large bowl, cream together the softened butter and sugar until light and fluffy.
   Add the eggs one at a time, beating well after each addition.
   Mix in the sour cream, dissolved yeast, and salt.
   Gradually add the flour, mixing until a soft dough forms. Knead the dough until it becomes smooth.
   Divide the dough into two equal portions.

2. Prepare the Fillings:

Poppy Seed Filling:

   In a saucepan, combine ground poppy seeds, milk, sugar, honey, butter, and lemon zest.
   Cook over medium heat, stirring constantly, until the mixture thickens. Remove from heat and let it cool.

Walnut Filling:

   In another saucepan, combine ground walnuts, milk, sugar, honey, butter, and orange zest.
   Cook over medium heat, stirring constantly, until the mixture thickens. Remove from heat and let it cool.

3. Roll Out the Dough:

   Preheat the oven to 350°F (180°C).
   Roll out one portion of the dough into a rectangle on a floured surface.

4. Add Fillings:

   Spread half of the poppy seed filling on one rectangle of dough.
   Roll it up into a log and place it on a parchment-lined baking sheet.
   Repeat the process with the other portion of dough and the walnut filling.

5. Brush with Egg Wash:

- Beat one egg and brush it over the tops of the rolls for a golden finish.

6. Bake:

- Bake in the preheated oven for about 30-35 minutes or until the rolls are golden brown.

7. Cool and Dust with Powdered Sugar:

- Allow the beigli rolls to cool completely before slicing.
- Dust with powdered sugar before serving.

Beigli is a delightful treat, and the combination of the poppy seed and walnut fillings provides a rich and festive flavor. Enjoy this Hungarian Christmas classic with friends and family!

Szaloncukor (Christmas Candy)

Ingredients:

- 2 cups granulated sugar
- 1 cup water
- 1 tablespoon white vinegar
- 1 tablespoon powdered sugar (for dusting)
- 1-2 teaspoons fruit-flavored extract (e.g., raspberry, orange, lemon)
- Food coloring (optional)
- Cornstarch (for dusting)

Instructions:

1. Prepare the Sugar Syrup:

   In a saucepan, combine sugar, water, and vinegar.
   Heat over medium heat, stirring until the sugar is completely dissolved.
   Bring the mixture to a boil, then reduce the heat and simmer for about 15-20 minutes, or until it reaches the soft-ball stage (about 235°F or 118°C on a candy thermometer).

2. Flavor the Syrup:

- Add 1-2 teaspoons of your chosen fruit-flavored extract to the syrup. Adjust the flavor to your liking.

3. Optional Coloring:

- If desired, add a few drops of food coloring to achieve the desired color for your candies.

4. Cool the Mixture:

- Allow the syrup to cool for a few minutes until it is comfortable to handle.

5. Form the Candies:

Dust a clean surface with cornstarch.
Using your hands, roll small portions of the syrup into bite-sized balls. The cornstarch will prevent sticking.

6. Let the Candies Dry:

- Place the formed candies on a tray or parchment paper to dry. Let them sit for at least a few hours or overnight.

7. Dust with Powdered Sugar:

- Once the candies are dry, dust them with powdered sugar to prevent sticking.

8. Store:

- Store Szaloncukor in a cool, dry place. They can be stored in an airtight container until ready to be enjoyed.

9. Display on the Christmas Tree:

- String a loop of thread through each candy, and hang them on the Christmas tree for a festive and edible decoration.

Szaloncukor can be made in various flavors, and the candies are often wrapped in colorful foil before being hung on the Christmas tree. They make for a sweet and decorative addition to the holiday season in Hungarian traditions.

www.ingramcontent.com/pod-product-compliance
Lightning Source LLC
LaVergne TN
LVHW081610060526
838201LV00054B/2172